# MY FIRST BOOK OF *Ballet*

Author   P M Rathbone

Photographs by Studio Styling

Scenario   Dance Studio

**H**ello! My name is Helen and on Wednesday afternoons I go to my ballet class. One day I want to be a ballerina. I change into a pink leotard, white tights and leather ballet shoes. These clothes give me more freedom to move. Boy dancers, like Tom, wear black leggings, a white tee-shirt, but no shoes.

I get changed quickly so that Mummy can put my hair in a bun. My teacher says that hair should not fall over my face. It is a bit chilly in the changing rooms so my friend, Anna, wears her 'cache-coeur'. This is the French word for an exercise cardigan. My teacher told me that ballet started in France and that is why so many of the exercises have French names. French is the language of ballet.

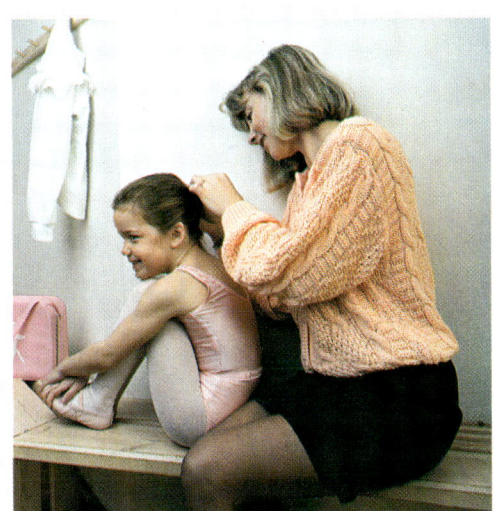

This is my teacher, the class calls her 'Madame'. She is very kind and always dances beautifully.
When I am grown up, I want to be as good a dancer as she is.

The whole class sits on the floor in a circle. Madame says, 'Keep your backs straight, relax your shoulders, stretch your legs and point your toes.' It is not easy, but we do this exercise to strengthen our backs.

**T**his is how you point your toes. Pull your toes down to the ground, but don't bend your knees! Julie's got it right! 'This exercise will strengthen your feet so that you can wear pointes when you are older,' says Madame.

**P**ointes are special ballet shoes with hardened toes that allow a dancer to dance on the tips of her toes. Madame pushes my toes down while holding my legs straight. That doesn't hurt, but it is a lot harder than it looks!

This is the next exercise on the floor. We have to try to push our knees to the ground while keeping our backs straight. Madame helps Anna to keep her knees flat.

Ow! This exercise is hard. 'Lean well forward, Helen,' says Madame. She pushes on my back. This exercise helps my muscles to become supple, but it is a bit painful.

This is a nice exercise. Tom and Julie put one foot against the other's and straighten their legs without letting go of their hands.

Now we make a crown by lifting our arms above our heads. Just like princes and princesses. I begin to think I am one! This position is called 'la couronne'.

Madame explains the next exercise to us. 'Keeping your backs straight, stretch out your legs to either side and then raise your arms above your heads in the crown position.'

It sounds easy, but...

Madame comes to help me. She pulls gently on my legs. 'Come on, Helen,' she says, 'just stretch your legs a little bit more. The more you try, the easier it will get.'

**A**nna watches as Karen and I lean forward between our legs with our toes pointed. We have to try to keep our backs as straight as possible and our legs facing forward. Phew! It is not easy, but Madame says it will make us supple.

After all those exercises, we try a dance on the floor. It is called the water lily. I lean over to the side, my hands on my feet, and my head on one side. I am supposed to be a leaf floating on the water. Anna is a leaf, too, and Julie is the flower, with a lovely halo crown.

**G**ood dancers always stand very straight. The feet are together, the stomach held in, the back straight, shoulders relaxed and the arms in the 'bras bas' position.

**F**or the last floor exercise we clap our hands to improve our rhythm. We listen carefully to the music and then clap the rhythm we have heard. Sometimes we take it in turns to do this. We like this exercise very much!

The first exercise at the barre is the 'plié', which means that we bend our legs. We stand with heels together and toes out to either side. Our hands are on the barre and our heads held up. Madame says, 'Demi-plié' and the music begins. One, two, three, four. 'Keep your knees over your toes when you bend your legs.' Five, six, seven, eight. Madame comes to help me when I have to do a 'grand-plié'.

The first things you learn when you start ballet are the five positions of the feet. It is very important for a dancer to know these in order to do the correct movements later on. We move our feet, but keep our arms in the 'bras bas' position.

Karen is in the first position. Her heels are together and her toes point to either side.

This is me, doing the second position. My toes point the same way, but my feet are apart.

Look at Anna in the third position. Here, one heel goes in front of the other.

Tom shows us the fourth position. One foot in front and the other a little bit behind it.

Julie is in the fifth position. The heel of one foot touches the toes of the foot behind.

The arms have different positions too. The 'bras bas' position is with the arms relaxed. The arms fall at your sides, but they are rounded. I am showing you the first position. My arms are rounded in front of me.

Anna shows us the second position. 'Keep your shoulders relaxed, but don't let your hands droop. And let me see you smile,' instructs Madame.

This is the best position. It is called 'la couronne'. You already know why, don't you? Madame helps Julie to keep her back straight and her stomach pulled in. I think this is the most beautiful position.

**A**nd now, the jumping exercise. We stand up straight, feet together and arms behind our backs. Madame counts. 'One, two, three.' We bend our legs in a demi-plié and when she says 'four' we jump as high as we can with our toes pointed and heads held up.

**N**ow we learn the 'demi-pointes' position. We must try to walk as high as we can on our toes, with legs straight. All the toes of each foot must touch the floor.

I love the improvisation exercise. Madame puts on some music and we can dance how we like. Sometimes we make up a little dance. See how Julie, Karen and Anna try out new steps on their own. Don't they look graceful?

**A**nna tries to balance in a difficult position. She has seen the older dancers practising it. Sometimes Madame does it too. I will try to balance like this soon.

**O**ur class has finished now. The older pupils are here. I want to stay and watch them. I enjoy watching them putting on their shoes and warming up.

See how much they know already! And their legs look so long and elegant when they point their toes!

I hurry over to the barre to join in with the older girls as they do their exercises. Hold the leg to one side, arm over the head and keep the stomach pulled in. Well, that's not so difficult! Don't you think I am as good as them? I am enjoying myself, but Madame claps her hands. 'Come on now, Helen,' she says, 'it's time to go home.' What a pity!

**I** curtsey to Madame, just like a real ballerina. 'See you next Wednesday, Helen,' she says, smiling. Tonight I will dance in my dreams. I will dream about Helen, the best ballerina in the world!

With thanks to Helen, Julie, Anna, Karen, Tom, Christine and Guy of the Dance Studio for their enthusiastic participation.
Also to Christian and Alain of Studio Styling.

The plants seen in these photographs are used for decoration only and are not normally part of the studio.

© 1991 by Invader Ltd., Chichester PO20 7EQ, England. All rights reserved.
Original edition: © 1991 by ZNU n.v., Belgium. All rights reserved.